All About Dinosaurs

Pterodactyl

Daniel Nunn

Heinemann
LIBRARY

Edited by Daniel Nunn and James Benefield
Designed by Tim Bond
Picture research by Tracy Cummins
Production by Helen McCreath
Originated by Capstone Global Library Ltd
Printed and bound in China by Leo Paper Group

18 17 16 15 14
10 9 8 7 6 5 4 3 2 1

Library of Congress Cataloging-in-Publication Data
Nunn, Daniel, author.
  Pterodactyl / Daniel Nunn.
    pages cm.—(All about dinosaurs)
  Includes bibliographical references and index.
  ISBN 978-1-4846-0205-8 (hb)—ISBN 978-1-4846-0212-6
(pb) 1. Pterodactyls—Juvenile literature. I. Title.

QE862.P7N86 2015
567.918—dc23   2013040466

Acknowledgments
We would like to thank the following for permission
to reproduce photographs: age footstock p. 10 (©
fotototo); Alamy pp. 8 (© Stocktrek Images, Inc.), 21 (©
Corbin17); Corbis p. 18 (© Kevin Schafer); Getty Images
pp. 7 (Andrew Kerr), 23 (Ulrich Baumgarten); istockphoto
p. 5 (© johan63); Photoshot p. 15 (Raymon Tercafs);
Science Source pp. 13 (Roger Harris), 20 (Tom McHugh);
Shutterstock 5a (Michael Rosskothen), 5b (Matt
Jeppson), 5c (Cathy Keifer), 7 background (mycola), 9
(Space-kraft), 11, 12, 14 (Michael Rosskothen), 16 (Vlada
Zhykharieva), 24 (tratong); Superstock pp. 4 (Stocktrek),
6 (Science Photo Library), 17 (Stocktrek Images), 19
(Universal Images Group).

Cover photograph of three Pteranodon Longicepts
flying, with two diplodocus dinosaurs near the shore,
with permission of Shutterstock (Linda Bucklin).

Back cover photograph of pterodactyl reproduced with
permission of Shutterstock (Michael Rosskothen).

We would like to thank Dee Reid and Nancy Harris for
their invaluable help in the preparation of this book.

Every effort has been made to contact copyright holders
of material reproduced in this book. Any omissions will
be rectified in subsequent printings if notice is given to
the publisher.

Contents

Meet the Pterodactyls

Pterodactyls lived long ago.

They are also called pterosaurs.

pterodactyl

snake

crocodile

lizard

Pterodactyls were reptiles.
Snakes, crocodiles, and lizards
are reptiles that live today.

Pteranodon

Some pterodactyls were big.
Pteranodon was big.

Pterodactylus

There were other types of pterodactyls. Pterodactylus was small.

What Were Pterodactyls Like?

wings

Pterodactyls had wings.

Pterodactyls could fly.

legs

Pterodactyls had four legs.

Pterodactyls could walk.

beak

Pterodactyls had long beaks.

Pterodactyls ate fish, insects, and small animals.

teeth

Some pterodactyls had teeth.

Some pterodactyls did not
have teeth.

Where Are Pterodactyls Now?

Pterodactyls are extinct. There are no pterodactyls alive now.

All the pterodactyls died long ago.

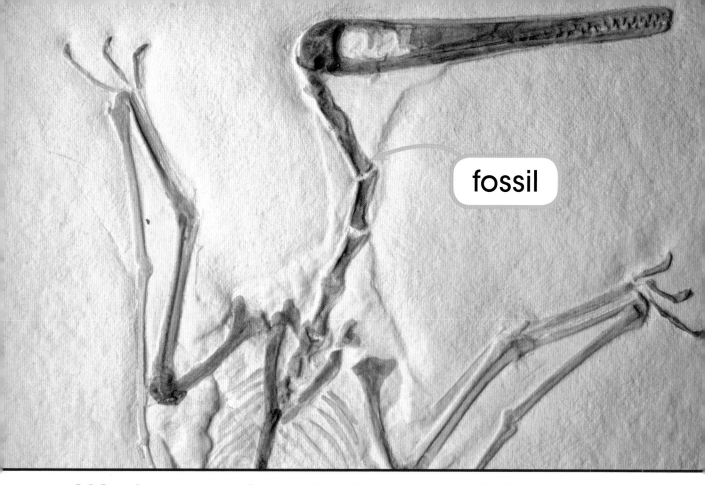

fossil

We learn about pterodactyls
from fossils.

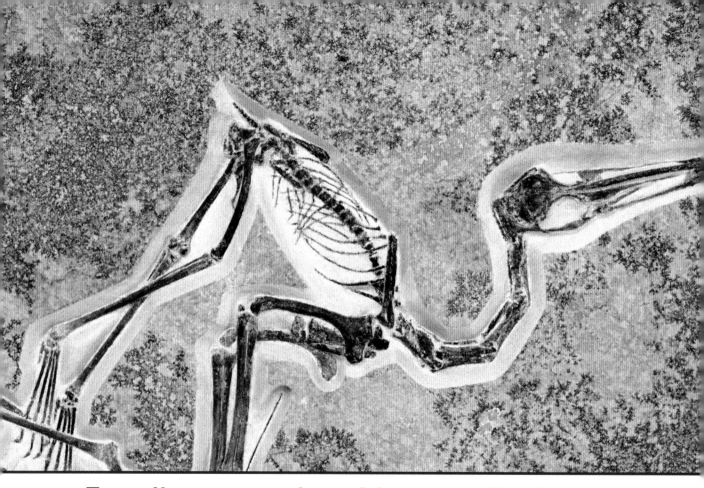

Fossils are animal bones that
have turned to rock.

People find fossils in the ground.

Fossils show us what pterodactyls looked like.

Where In the World?

Pterodactyl fossils have
been found all over the world.

Picture Glossary

fossil animal bones or parts of a plant that have turned into rock

reptile cold-blooded animal. A lizard is a reptile.

How to Say It

Pteranodon: say "terr-arn-uh-don"

Pterodactyl: say "terr-uh-dak-til"

Pterodactylus: say "terr-uh-dak-til-us"

Index

Notes for Parents and Teachers

Before reading

Ask the children to name some dinosaurs. Ask them if dinosaurs are around today. Have they heard of pterodactyls? Explain that pterodactyls were not dinosaurs, but they lived at the same time as dinosaurs. Find out if they already know about pterodactyls.

After reading

- Choose some fast music and ask the children to fly like pterodactyls. Show them how to flap their arms and then hold them still as they glide. Ask the children to imagine they are diving to catch a fish. Then ask them to walk like a pterodactyl on the land.
- Ask the children to draw pterodactyls flying with outstretched wings. Get them to cut out their drawings and hang them from the classroom ceiling, so that they fly above the children's heads.

12/14